The **INSIDE GUIDE**

FAMOUS NATIVE AMERICANS

Crazy Horse

By Jodyanne Benson

Cavendish Square

New York

Published in 2021 by Cavendish Square Publishing, LLC
243 5th Avenue, Suite 136, New York, NY 10016

Copyright © 2021 by Cavendish Square Publishing, LLC

First Edition

Library of Congress Cataloging-in-Publication Data

Names: Benson, Jodyanne, author.
Title: Crazy Horse / Jodyanne Benson.
Description: First edition. | New York, NY : Cavendish Square Publishing,
LLC, 2021. | Series: The inside guide: famous Native Americans | Includes
bibliographical references and index.
Identifiers: LCCN 2019042516 (print) | LCCN 2019042517 (ebook) | ISBN
9781502650542 (library binding) | ISBN 9781502650528 (paperback) | ISBN
9781502650535 (set) | ISBN 9781502650559 (ebook)
Subjects: LCSH: Crazy Horse, approximately 1842-1877–Juvenile literature.
| Oglala Indians–Kings and rulers–Biography–Juvenile literature. |
Oglala Indians–History–Juvenile literature. | Indians of North
America–Great Plains–Wars–Juvenile literature.
Classification: LCC E99.O3 B46 2021 (print) | LCC E99.O3 (ebook) | DDC
978.004/9752440092 [B]–dc23
LC record available at https://lccn.loc.gov/2019042516
LC ebook record available at https://lccn.loc.gov/2019042517

Editor: Kristen Susienka
Copy Editor: Rebecca Rohan
Designer: Deanna Paternostro

Find us on

CONTENTS

Native American tribes are led by chiefs, like the Lakota Sioux chiefs shown here.

LEGENDARY HEROES

Throughout the history of the United States, many men and women stand out for their bravery, skills, determination, or success. Sometimes, their stories become legends for a group of Americans.

Among these people are Native Americans. They were the first people to live in what we now call the United States. Before any big cities were built, skyscrapers reached for the heavens, or railroads and planes moved people around the country, Native Americans formed their own societies. They had families and protectors and wise people leading them. They farmed, fished, hunted, celebrated, and mourned. Today, they continue to be part of the many people who make up America.

Fast Fact

Many Native American communities were led by people working together. A group, or council, of elders helped make decisions and passed down a tribe's history and legends. Elders still play an important part in native **culture** today.

Many Native Americans became expert horse riders and fighters on horseback. They first learned of horses when the Spanish introduced them to North America in the 1500s.

Native Americans were very good at hunting bison on horseback.

Honor and Remembrance

Today, many native people are celebrated. Some people are well known, like Pocahontas or Sacagawea. Others might be new names to you, like Sequoyah or Crazy Horse. Learning about them gives you the chance to get to know different people who lived during different times in US history. They left marks on their communities, and we can still learn from their stories today.

Fast Fact

Crazy Horse did a lot in his short life. Although his exact birthday isn't known, he's thought to have been between 28 and 35 years old when he died.

The first Thanksgiving feast is imagined here. It's remembered today as a time when settlers from Europe and Native Americans came together to celebrate a good harvest.

ORAL TRADITION

For a long time, Native American groups didn't have languages that were written down. Instead, Native Americans told stories to each other from memory. This was how they passed their stories on from one generation to the next. Men and women told the stories to the children of their tribe. The tales talked about important people and events; everyday things like weaving, hunting, or fishing; and the values of the tribe.

This way of passing down history is called oral tradition. "Oral" means "by word of mouth." Storytellers were very important to many ancient groups of people, not just Native Americans. Some of the most well-known stories told from oral tradition and later written down are the Greek myths and the Anansi tales from Africa.

Today, storytellers still matter. Telling stories is a way to spark a person's imagination or to get them to remember key information quickly. In communities around the world, stories connect people to each other. Oral tradition is still alive in some groups of people. It offers people the chance to celebrate history while also keeping traditions alive.

A tribe's history and beliefs were passed down from elders to younger generations through storytelling.

Crazy Horse

One of the most well-known Native Americans from the 1800s was Crazy Horse. He led his people against US troops that wanted the land on which Crazy Horse and his people lived. This desire for land was part of an idea called **Manifest Destiny**. Crazy Horse refused to give up. He died a hero to his people and is remembered today in many ways. Read on to learn more about Crazy Horse's life and accomplishments!

Many actors have played Crazy Horse in movies. This is how actor Michael Greyeyes looked when he played the part.

This artwork shows Crazy Horse fighting US general George Custer.

THE LIFE OF CRAZY HORSE

Crazy Horse was a popular Native American leader and warrior who lived in the mid-to-late 1800s. He's most well known for fighting American soldiers during a time when Native Americans were forced off of much of their land. He's also known as a kind and giving man toward members of his tribe. He's still a hero to many today.

Who Was Crazy Horse?

Crazy Horse was born around 1842 in what's now South Dakota. He was a Lakota chief. The Lakota were part of the Sioux nation. Crazy Horse was a brave and smart warrior. He protected his people and home in the **Great Plains**.

Fast Fact

Whenever Crazy Horse fought a battle, he wore a feather in his hair. His face was painted with the symbol of a lightning bolt. These things were thought to protect him in a fight.

THE OGLALA LAKOTA

In Native American culture, several smaller tribes make up larger tribes. Crazy Horse lived for a long time with a smaller tribe in the Lakota group of Native Americans called the Oglala (pronounced oh-GLAH-lah). However, his actual heritage was through a different band of Lakota, the Minnikojou. Since Crazy Horse lived so long with the Oglala tribe, though, it's important to know the group's history.

Based on stories from Oglala elders, it's been said that the Oglala tribe formed in the 1700s. They lived in tents made from bison skin. The tents were called tepees. Women in the tribe took care of the home. They made food and clothes. Men were warriors and hunters. Once the tribe had horses, they gave up farming to follow and hunt bison. Both men and women were storytellers, artists, and musicians.

In Crazy Horse's time, the Oglala had their own rules, traditions, and beliefs. Some of these practices have changed over time, while others are the same. Today, the tribe still exists. It has its own government, laws, and police. People live in houses and apartments. Most live on the Pine Ridge Indian **Reservation** in South Dakota. They continue telling stories and making art and music.

A Lakota camp, complete with horses and tepees, stretches over the plains.

The Early Years

Crazy Horse's mother was named Rattling Blanket Woman. The women of his family raised him. With their help, he became a model member of their society.

Crazy Horse's father was a medicine man and was also named Crazy Horse. Later, he was called Waglula, which means "Worm." Crazy Horse took on his father's name later in life. His Lakota birth name was Chan Ohan. It means "Among the Trees." As a boy, he didn't look like others in his tribe. His curly hair made him different.

When he was old enough, Crazy Horse went on a vision quest. He went into the mountains for four days and prayed. After the vision quest, Crazy Horse was considered an adult in his tribe.

Crazy Horse grew up when America

Fast Fact

Medicine men were healers and spiritual leaders in native communities.

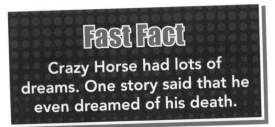
was changing. New technologies, like trains, made it easier for people in the eastern part of the United States to travel across North America. Soon, settlers were moving into Lakota territory.

Battle of the Little Bighorn

In the 1850s and 1860s, the United States and the Lakota didn't get along. The United States had grown a lot, and the government wanted more land. It also wanted more white settlers to live in the area of the country where the Lakota were. The Lakota fought for the right to keep their land free from settlers.

Crazy Horse was a warrior who fought many battles. The US Army believed he was very dangerous. Crazy Horse did everything he could to protect his tribe and his way of life.

This worked for a time. However, in 1874, gold was discovered in the Black Hills of South Dakota. This area was where the Lakota lived. The US government sent settlers to Lakota territory. They wanted gold and land. Settlers set up towns and moved their families into houses they built there. The Lakota watched this happen and tried to resist, but soon the government ordered all Lakota onto reservations.

Crazy Horse didn't want to go to a reservation. On June 17, 1876, he led more than 1,000 Oglala and **Cheyenne** men to fight against a US general named George Crook and his army. They forced the army to turn around.

On June 25, 1876, Crazy Horse and his friend Chief Sitting Bull joined their armies

Settlers and Native Americans fought over gold found in mines like this one in South Dakota.

This painting shows the Battle of the Little Bighorn in June 1876. It took place near the Little Bighorn River in Montana Territory.

to defeat US Army officer George A. Custer and his troops. This fight was called the Battle of the Little Bighorn or Custer's Last Stand. Crazy Horse showed great bravery in the fight. Twice he charged into battle and never got hurt. In the end, the native armies won. It was a great victory for them and gave them hope they could save their way of life.

The Death of Crazy Horse

However, it was too difficult to fight the US Army forever. On May 6, 1877, Crazy Horse **surrendered** at Fort Robinson in Nebraska, which was part of the Red Cloud Agency reservation. He didn't follow orders to stay on the reservation, though. Some stories say that during the summer, he left to take his sick wife to her parents at another reservation. Other stories differ. However, it's known that he was arrested and returned to Fort Robinson. He fought with the officers there and was killed on September 5, 1877.

Railroads brought a lot of settlers to the American West. They provided easy transportation and jobs.

CHANGES ON THE GREAT PLAINS

In the 1800s, when Crazy Horse lived, many white people wanted to move to the western United States. They heard stories of gold, land for farming, and other things in the West that could make them rich. Many white people in the United States also believed in Manifest Destiny. They thought it was their right to control all the land from coast to coast.

When white people did move west, they didn't think about the Lakota or other Native Americans. They thought native people weren't as smart or as important as them because they had different homes, traditions, and beliefs. The land the Lakota had always lived on was slowly taken from them through a series of **treaties**. This changing life for the Lakota played a big part in the story of Crazy Horse.

A Changing Life for the Lakota

In the 1800s, settlers started entering Lakota territory. They wanted to hunt there. Hunting animals for their fur was a popular thing to do. Fur made

Fast Fact

Many wild bison roamed the West when Crazy Horse was growing up. However, settlers hunted them, and by 1884, there were only 325 wild bison left in the United States.

warm clothing for people to wear in tough winter weather. It also looked nice on walls or used as rugs. Settlers killed many animals. Many bison that lived on Lakota land were hunted.

For years, the Lakota had followed and hunted the bison. They made sure to use every part of the animal, not just its fur. Once settlers started killing all of the bison, there weren't enough bison for the Lakota. The Native Americans struggled to survive.

Losing Trust in the United States

Settlers and Native Americans didn't always get along. There were many fights and arguments. One fight happened in August 1854. A man named John Grattan brought a group of soldiers into a Sioux camp. They wanted to arrest men they thought had stolen a settler's cow. The Sioux chief, named Conquering Bear, wouldn't give in. The soldiers killed the chief. The tribe fought back and killed Grattan and his men. Settlers who heard the story feared the native people more. For young Crazy Horse, hearing about this event made him wonder if he could ever trust settlers.

This image shows wagons and oxen carrying settlers West in the 1800s.

Big Problems

Treaties created problems between Native Americans and the US government. Treaties would promise one thing, then settlers would do another, breaking that promise. Tribes grew to distrust the white men. One such treaty was the First Treaty of Fort Laramie of 1851. It alarmed many native communities living in the West. A law called the Homestead Act of 1862 also worried Native Americans. Both took away land from the tribes that once had been promised to them.

Thousands of Sioux and Cheyenne warriors hid behind a hill before attacking Captain Fetterman and his soldiers.

Beginning in 1865, Crazy Horse and his people fought with the US government. The problem started when the government wanted to build a road in Montana. Military forts were also to be built along the road. Crazy Horse did many things to show the government he wasn't happy with this plan. On December 21, 1866, he was part of the **massacre** of Captain William J. Fetterman and his troops. Crazy Horse also took part in a battle called the Wagon Box Fight on August 2, 1867. Events like these made both Native Americans and settlers angry and upset.

In 1868, the Second Treaty of Fort Laramie made new borders and reservations for Native Americans. The US government took control of Native American lands. The government gave the Native Americans in

A PERFECT TEAM

Sitting Bull was another Lakota chief. He united and led the Sioux tribes in their struggle to protect their home on the Great Plains.

Crazy Horse and Sitting Bull were both strong leaders. However, they were very different. Crazy Horse was quiet. Sitting Bull was good at talking to large groups of people. Together, they made a good team and gave their people strength.

Sitting Bull was also a Lakota chief.

the West a new place to live. One part of this agreement formed the large Great Sioux Reservation in what are now the states of South Dakota and Nebraska. However, Crazy Horse refused to live on a reservation at that time.

The Final Fight

The Second Treaty of Fort Laramie in 1868 said the Sioux (the larger nation to which the Lakota belonged) could live on the Black Hills in South Dakota. The Black Hills were very important to the Sioux. This made the Sioux happy, but it didn't last long.

In 1874, miners looking for gold settled on the **sacred** land. The Lakota were angry, but they couldn't get the settlers to go away. They also didn't want to sell the land to the United States.

The US government then ordered that all Native Americans had to live on reservations by January 31, 1876. Soldiers would fight any Native Americans who didn't follow this order. Crazy Horse was one who didn't listen. He joined Chief Sitting Bull to fight the US Army. In 1877, though, the Sioux gave up their rights to the Black Hills, and many moved to reservations. Eventually, Crazy Horse and others who resisted either moved or were killed trying to protect their way of life.

Fast Fact

The Black Hills are still important to the Lakota today. In fact, the Lakota consider them the center of the world.

For the Sioux, the Black Hills in South Dakota are important not just for resources. The Black Hills are part of their history and tradition.

The Lakota Sioux
tribe still keeps many
traditional customs,
like dancing at events
called powwows.

REMEMBERING CRAZY HORSE

Crazy Horse is remembered as a great fighter who played an important part in the Battle of the Little Bighorn, but his story is much more than that. It lives on today in the Lakota tribe, which he fought to save.

Crazy Horse's Legacy

Today, Crazy Horse's legacy is part of Lakota life. "Legacy" means memories or ideas that someone in the past leaves after he or she dies. Crazy Horse left a legacy of strength and determination.

He became a hero not just because he was a strong fighter. He was also a protector and stood up for his people. He was a role model for others, which means he was someone for others to look up to.

After Crazy Horse died, people began to tell his story. Many people learned about his bravery. He had done everything he could to **preserve** the Lakota way of life. Many Lakota liked Crazy Horse because he wouldn't give in when faced with challenges.

The Crazy Horse Memorial

A memorial is usually a stone structure built in memory of someone or something. People can visit a memorial in honor of that person or event.

Memorials can teach us a lot about history. Crazy Horse is remembered with a memorial.

The Crazy Horse Memorial is carved into the top of a mountain in the beautiful Black Hills in South Dakota. It shows Crazy Horse riding a horse and pointing into the distance. Since there are no pictures of Crazy Horse, it's not what he looked like exactly. It's what people think he might have looked like, though we can never be sure.

A Lakota elder named Henry Standing Bear first thought of the idea for the monument. He and other elders asked sculptor Korczak Ziolkowski to sculpt it. Work on the memorial started in 1948. Ziolkowski spent almost half his life working on it. After Ziolkowski died, his wife and children continued work on it. The giant carving still isn't finished. When it's done, it will be 641 feet (195 meters) long and 563 feet (172 m) high. The entire memorial also includes a museum and learning center.

Fast Fact

Crazy Horse never had his picture taken. People today wonder what he looked like.

Not everyone is happy about the memorial. Some people don't see Crazy Horse as a figure worth remembering. To some, he was a troublemaker who damaged relationships between his tribe

The Crazy Horse Memorial is being carved into a mountain in the Black Hills.

IN THE FOOTSTEPS OF CRAZY HORSE

Crazy Horse has inspired many books. Long biographies like *Crazy Horse: The Lakota Warrior's Life and Legacy* explore for adult audiences what Crazy Horse's life was like, as told by his relatives. Other stories examine Crazy Horse's tale in other ways. One example is *In the Footsteps of Crazy Horse*, written by Joseph M. Marshall III. This book is for young readers. It follows a young Lakota boy named Jimmy and his grandfather as they take a trip. Jimmy has light skin and hair and doesn't feel like he looks like others on his reservation. His grandfather thinks of Crazy Horse, who also looked different from his tribe. On their trip, Jimmy's grandfather tells the wonderful stories that shaped Crazy Horse's life. The book tells American history from the Lakota perspective. It helps others understand what Crazy Horse was like and how important it is to be proud of your differences.

Joseph Marshall III is known for his books on the life of Crazy Horse.

and the US government during his life. No matter what people may think, everyone can learn from visiting the memorial.

Crazy Horse's relatives are also still living today and carrying on his memory. They published a book about Crazy Horse's life in 2016. It's called *Crazy Horse: The Lakota's Life and Legacy*. The stories in it were told over several generations. His great-nephew Edward Clown and other authors of the book help paint a more **accurate** picture of who Crazy Horse was and how he changed history.

There may not be pictures of Crazy Horse, but his life story has many moments that help us imagine who he was. Crazy Horse's story is remembered by the Lakota and shared with others today. For the Lakota and many others, stories and memories of the man are treasured, just like a photograph of someone who is gone.

THINK ABOUT IT!

Use these questions to help you think more deeply about this topic.

1. How do you think Crazy Horse should be remembered?

2. What can Crazy Horse's life teach us about being different from those around us?

3. How did life change for many Native Americans living in the West from the 1850s to the 1870s?

4. When was the first transcontinental railroad finished, and how did it affect Native Americans?

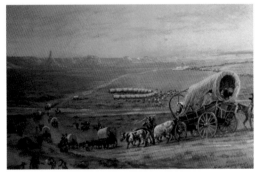

5. What is different and special about Crazy Horse's memorial?

TIMELINE

Crazy Horse's Life	World Events

1842
This may be the year Crazy Horse is born near present-day Rapid City, South Dakota.

1866
Crazy Horse participates in the massacre of Captain William J. Fetterman and his troops.

1868
The Second Treaty of Fort Laramie promises the Black Hills to the Sioux.

1876
The Battle of the Little Bighorn takes place.

1877
Crazy Horse dies at Fort Robinson in Nebraska.

1849
About 80,000 people travel to California searching for gold.

1861–1865
The American Civil War is fought between the Union army and the Confederate States of America.

1862
The signing of the Homestead Act of 1862 makes it easier for settlers to claim and buy land in the West.

1869
The first transcontinental railroad in the United States is finished, connecting the East and West.

1884
Only 325 wild bison are alive in the United States.

GLOSSARY

accurate: Right or true.

Cheyenne: A group of Native Americans who lived around the Platte and Arkansas Rivers during the 19th century and still exist today.

culture: The beliefs and ways of life of a group of people.

Great Plains: An area of flat land that is west of the Mississippi River and east of the Rocky Mountains in North America.

Manifest Destiny: The idea that the United States should expand from one coast to the other because it was the country's God-given right.

massacre: The violent killing of many people.

preserve: To protect or keep safe from loss.

reservation: An area of land in the United States that is kept separate for Native Americans to live.

sacred: Special or important, especially in a religious sense.

surrender: To agree to stop fighting and give control to the opposing side.

treaty: An agreement that is made between two or more groups.

FIND OUT MORE

Books

Coleman, Miriam. *The Life of Crazy Horse*. New York, NY: PowerKids Press, 2016.

Marshall, Joseph M., III. *In the Footsteps of Crazy Horse*. New York, NY: Abrams, 2015.

Pascal, Janet B. *What Was the Wild West?* New York, NY: Penguin Random House, 2017.

Websites

Black Hills and Badlands, SD
www.blackhillsbadlands.com
Visit this website to learn more about the sacred Black Hills and surrounding area in South Dakota.

Britannica Kids: Crazy Horse
kids.britannica.com/kids/article/Crazy-Horse/353011
This educational website features a brief biography about Crazy Horse.

10 Famous Native Americans
history.howstuffworks.com/historical-figures/10-famous-native-americans.htm
This website gives mini biographies and a countdown of the top 10 famous Native Americans in US history.

INDEX